Space Scientist

TELESCOPES
AND OBSERVATORIES

Heather Couper and Nigel Henbest

Franklin Watts

London   New York   Toronto   Sydney

© 1987 Franklin Watts

First published in 1987 by
Franklin Watts
12a Golden Square
London W1R 4BA

First published in the USA
by Franklin Watts Inc.
387 Park Avenue South
New York, N.Y. 10016

First published in Australia
by Franklin Watts
Australia
14 Mars Road
Lane Cove, NSW 2066

UK ISBN: 0 86313 527 7
US ISBN: 0-531-10361-7
Library of Congress
Catalog Card No:
86-51415

Illustrations by
Drawing Attention
Rhoda Burns
Rob Burns
Eagle Artists
Michael Roffe

Photographs by
Hencoup Enterprises Ltd
Doug Johnson
Max Planck Institute for
Radio Astronomy
Robin Scagell
Science Photo Library

Designed by
David Jefferis

Printed in Belgium

Space Scientist

TELESCOPES
AND OBSERVATORIES

Contents

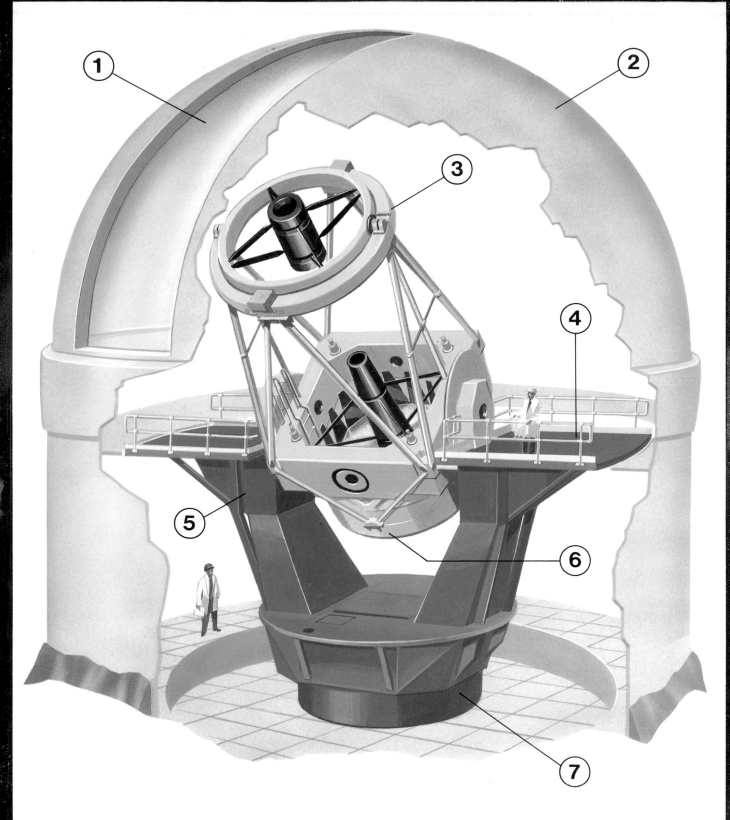

△ The William Herschel Telescope in La Palma, Canary Islands, is the world's third largest telescope.

1 Dome slit opens each night to allow the telescope to view the sky.

2 Protective dome acts as a windshield.

3 Lightweight skeleton tube.

4 Observation platform where scientific instruments are placed.

5 Massive yoke prevents the telescope from vibrating.

6 Main mirror 4.2 m (165 in) in diameter.

7 Computer-driven mounting enables the telescope to follow an object as the Earth rotates. The dome slit moves at the same time.

Eyes on the sky

People almost always associate telescopes with astronomers. But up until 400 years ago, astronomers observed the sky with their eyes alone. Then, thanks to a chance discovery made by a Dutch optician, Hans Lippershey, that a combination of two particular kinds of lens made distant objects appear closer, astronomers could at last home in on the objects they had gazed upon from afar.

Galileo, the first astronomer to make a proper record of his observations, discovered all kinds of things with his telescope. He saw craters on the Moon, four moons circling Jupiter, and he found that the misty band of the Milky Way was due to light from countless stars.

Telescopes not only allow you to see further; they let you see fainter objects, too. In many ways they're like giant eyes, picking up far more light than the human eye ever can. Today's huge "light buckets" photograph stars millions of times fainter than those we see.

But collecting light is just part of the story; it's what happens afterwards that counts. At a modern observatory, astronomers very seldom actually *look* through the telescopes. It's much more important to keep a permanent record of the light that's captured — either by taking a long-exposure photograph of the object the telescope is pointing at, or (as is more usual today) by storing the data electronically.

This, though, is just the beginning. Starlight comes to us as a kind of message, and valuable information is locked up in it. A great deal of an astronomer's job lies in decoding this message, by electronically scanning an image, or by splitting up light into its range of energies with an instrument called a *spectroscope*.

Light, however, is just one part of a much bigger story. Although giant telescopes reveal far more about the heavens than our eyes could ever do, most objects out in space emit other radiations that are invisible to us. To get the whole picture, you need to "tune in" to these other radiations, too; and thanks to advances in technology, today's astronomers can.

And so, when astronomers talk about their "observatory", it's just as likely that they are referring to a satellite picking up cosmic X-rays, or to a radio telescope, as to a conventional telescope under a dome.

◁ Perched on high mountains, under the darkest, clearest skies, the world's great observatories often have as many as a dozen big telescopes in use every night. Most are studying objects that are too faint to be visible to the naked eye.

▷ Today's telescopes can capture "invisible" radiations as well as light. This 100-m (330-ft)-diameter dish in Effelsberg, Germany, picks up cosmic radio waves. It's the world's largest fully steerable radio telescope.

The invisible Universe

Living without light seems almost impossible to us. But, astronomically speaking, light is one chapter of a much bigger story: it's just a tiny part of a huge spread of electrical and magnetic vibrations which make up the *electromagnetic spectrum*. We call these vibrations radiation.

One way to imagine the electromagnetic spectrum is as a piano keyboard. Light corresponds to the notes right in the middle: the chord of middle C. Some radiations, like infrared radiation and radio waves, have a "lower pitch" than light. Others — like ultraviolet radiation, X-rays, and gamma rays — make up the "high notes" of the keyboard. Most objects in the Universe "play" on all the notes. But, until very recently, we couldn't tune in to the bass and treble parts: we were limited to hearing the tune played only on middle C.

The vibrations making up the electromagnetic spectrum don't actually give out any sounds. But although they all travel forward at the same speed — the speed of light (300,000 km/sec) — each vibration has a "beat" it keeps time to. X-rays, for instance, vibrate very quickly; the "wiggle" (*wavelength*) of the vibration is very short. Radio waves, on the other hand, vibrate slowly; they are said to have a long wavelength.

The reason why we've only just succeeded in tuning into *all* the radiations lies in the Earth's atmosphere. Generally speaking, our atmosphere lets in long-wavelength radiation from space (light, some infrared, most radio waves), while blocking short-wavelength radiation. This is just as well for life on Earth: ultraviolet radiation, X-rays and gamma rays are *very* energetic and can even kill! However, it has meant that we weren't able to tune into any of these radiations until we could launch rockets and satellites above the atmosphere.

Nowadays, thanks to huge advances in electronics, computers and spaceprobe design, we can listen to the whole cosmic keyboard. But light's message is still of the greatest significance to astronomers — as you'll see in the next few pages.

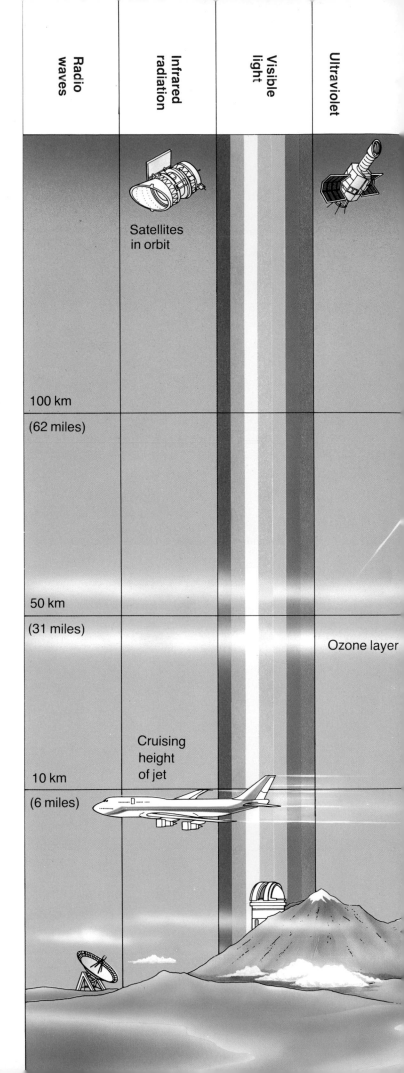

Radio waves

Infrared radiation

Visible light

Ultraviolet

Satellites in orbit

100 km
(62 miles)

50 km
(31 miles)

Ozone layer

Cruising height of jet

10 km
(6 miles)

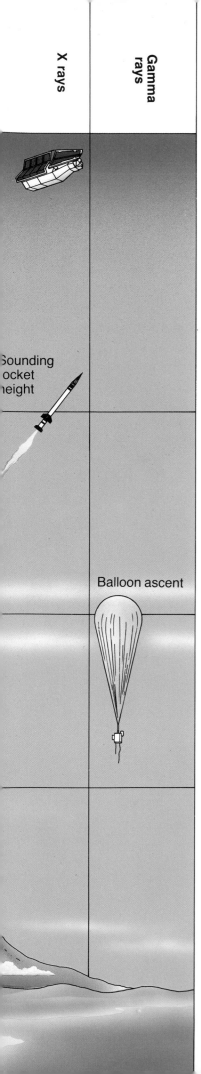

Sounding
rocket
height

Balloon ascent

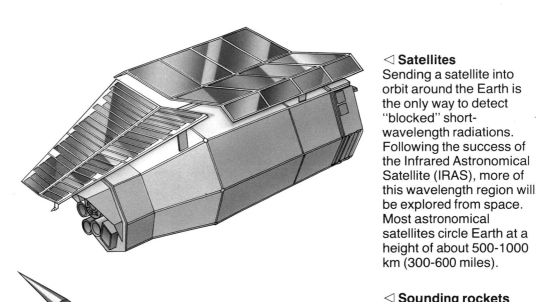

◁ Satellites
Sending a satellite into orbit around the Earth is the only way to detect "blocked" short-wavelength radiations. Following the success of the Infrared Astronomical Satellite (IRAS), more of this wavelength region will be explored from space. Most astronomical satellites circle Earth at a height of about 500-1000 km (300-600 miles).

◁ Sounding rockets
When astronomers began studying short-wave radiations, sounding rockets were the only means of getting instruments above the atmosphere. These rockets reach 100 km (60 miles) before falling back; the instrument payload parachutes back separately. A sounding rocket first detected cosmic X-rays in 1962.

◁ Balloons
Balloons, which can reach heights of 50 km (30 miles) before blowing up in the thin air, are much cheaper than rockets or satellites. They are used for experiments that need to get above nearly all of the atmosphere. They're especially useful for research into gamma rays — which penetrate the middle levels of the atmosphere — and infrared radiation.

◁ Observatories
Only visible light and radio waves (and, to a much lesser extent, infrared radiation) can penetrate all the way through the atmosphere and down to the ground. But to get above the pollution in the atmosphere — and the clouds — it's best that optical (light-gathering) observatories are sited on the highest mountains possible. Radio telescopes, on the other hand, can observe through cloud, but they need settled conditions to work best.

Gathering light

Although many people think that a telescope's main purpose is to magnify, this isn't actually true. Its function is to gather light. The bigger the telescope's collecting area — its lens or mirror — the more light it will collect, and the fainter (and further) it will see.

Early telescopes, like those first used by the Italian astronomer Galileo in 1608, were very small. They were all *refractors*: telescopes which gather light with a combination of lenses. But — like raindrops — lenses bend light, and create tiny "rainbows" around objects being viewed.

Isaac Newton (of gravity fame) hit on the solution less than a century later. He designed a telescope which gathered light with a concave mirror, like a shaving mirror, instead of a lens. Nowadays, all the world's major telescopes are *reflectors* like this. Reflectors have other advantages, too: because light only hits the mirror's front surface, it's relatively easy to support even a big, heavy mirror at the back. But a lens much more than a metre (40 in) across would sag under its own weight.

The world's biggest telescopes are the 6-m (236-in) Soviet reflector in the Caucasus Mountains; the Hale 5-m (200-in) reflector in California; and Britain's 4.2-m (165-in) William Herschel Telescope on La Palma in the Canary Islands. (The measurement refers to the mirror's diameter.) Computers help them to track the stars automatically as the Earth turns.

But astronomers are looking forward to the late 1980s, when the Hubble Space Telescope goes into orbit around the Earth. High above our churning, blurring atmosphere, this 2.4-m (94-in) reflector will see further and more penetratingly than any telescope before. It is bound to make many new discoveries.

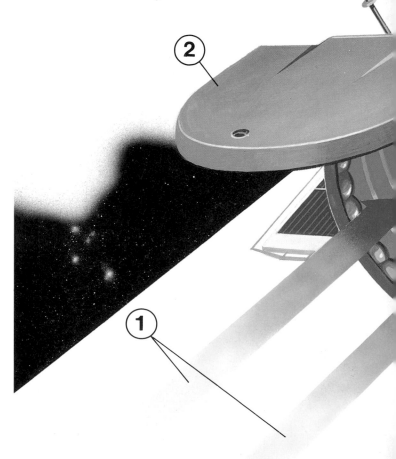

△ Isaac Newton's reflecting telescope had a mirror only 7.5 cm (3 in) across; but the world's biggest telescopes, and the Hubble Space Telescope (*right*), are based on his design. The HST will be launched late in 1988. But astronomers will still continue to use telescopes on the ground.

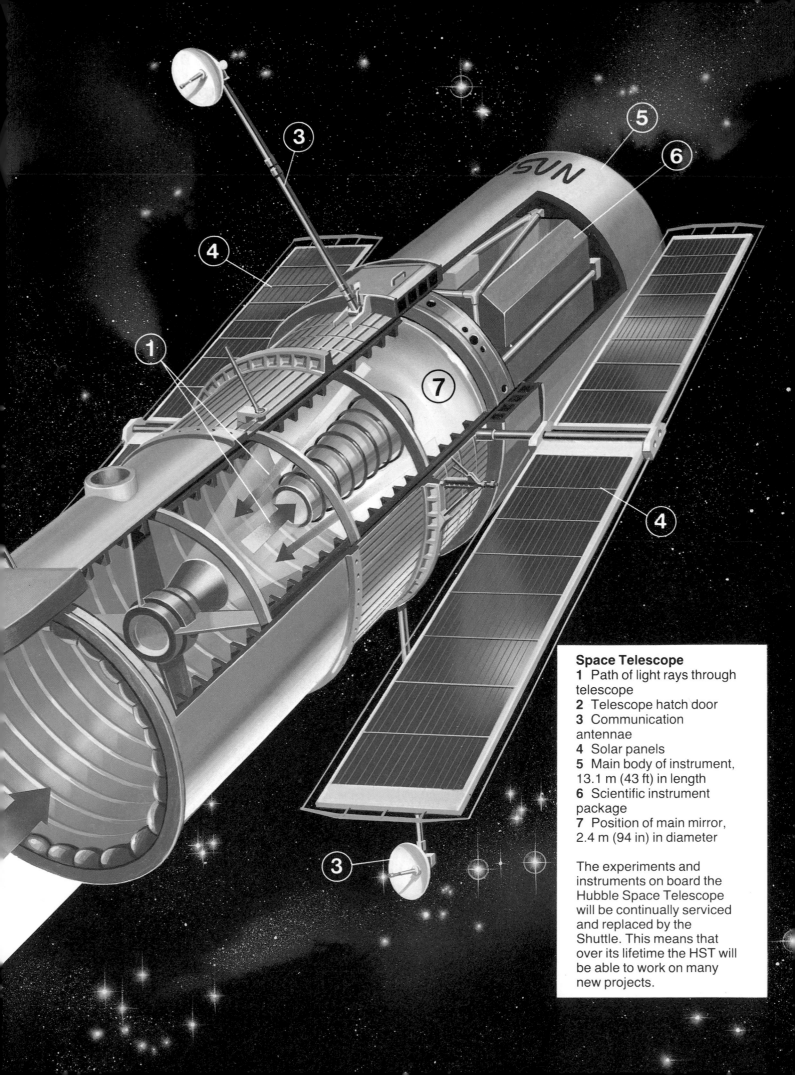

SUN

Space Telescope
1 Path of light rays through telescope
2 Telescope hatch door
3 Communication antennae
4 Solar panels
5 Main body of instrument, 13.1 m (43 ft) in length
6 Scientific instrument package
7 Position of main mirror, 2.4 m (94 in) in diameter

The experiments and instruments on board the Hubble Space Telescope will be continually serviced and replaced by the Shuttle. This means that over its lifetime the HST will be able to work on many new projects.

△ This 1910 photograph of Halley's Comet has been computer-enhanced (*top*) to bring out fine details not visible in the original. The old picture shows structure in the comet's tail, but not in the head. To reveal hidden structure, the photograph of the head was scanned with a small spot, and the electronic images were added together by computer. In the resulting colour-coded image, the different levels of brightness are shown by colours; you can also see a small jet to the left of centre not visible in the original.

△ This conventional photograph of the Orion Nebula (*above*) shows the faint outer gas streamers, but at the expense of revealing structure in the inner regions, which have been overexposed. The technique of unsharp masking reveals detail right across the nebula (*right*). This involves re-photographing the picture through a negative "mask" of itself.

Electronic eyes

Catching light with a telescope that's as big as possible is just part of an astronomer's job. What matters is what you *do* with all the light!

Until quite recently, most telescopes worked mainly as giant cameras, focusing their captured light on to a photographic plate. A long-exposure photograph reveals far more detail than the eye can ever glimpse. In fact, some telescopes (Schmidt telescopes) *only* operate as cameras, and are specially designed to photograph large areas of the sky.

Although photography is still important in astronomy, it isn't the most efficient way of recording light. More than nine-tenths of the hard-won light hitting a plate doesn't take part in the photographic process at all.

Luckily, electronics — and in particular, the *photoelectric effect* — come to the rescue. When a beam of light hits certain metals, it causes a stream of subatomic particles called electrons to be ejected. Together, these tiny, negatively charged particles make up an electric current. This current can be easily amplified to provide a

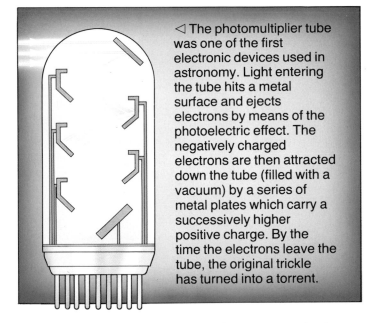

◁ The photomultiplier tube was one of the first electronic devices used in astronomy. Light entering the tube hits a metal surface and ejects electrons by means of the photoelectric effect. The negatively charged electrons are then attracted down the tube (filled with a vacuum) by a series of metal plates which carry a successively higher positive charge. By the time the electrons leave the tube, the original trickle has turned into a torrent.

strong signal — even when there's very little light coming in.

Most of today's electronic detectors take pictures, too. Some — *image intensifiers* — work rather like television cameras. But the most common detector of all is a tiny chip of light-sensitive silicon called a *charge-coupled device* (CCD).

Detectors like these have revolutionized astronomy. Photographic exposures that once took hours take only minutes with a CCD; and astronomers no longer have to sit in the cold all night checking that all is well.

But that's not the end of the story. Even when you've taken your pictures, you can still get more information out of them. You can improve photographs by a technique called unsharp masking, which brings out fine details washed out in the original. And electronic pictures can be processed by computer to bring out any aspect an astronomer wants — like faint rings around a planet, for instance. In fact, it's just as common today to see electronic pictures in "false colour", rather than true colour. Colour-coding is used to highlight different parts of the image — perhaps where there are different processes going on.

Light's hidden message

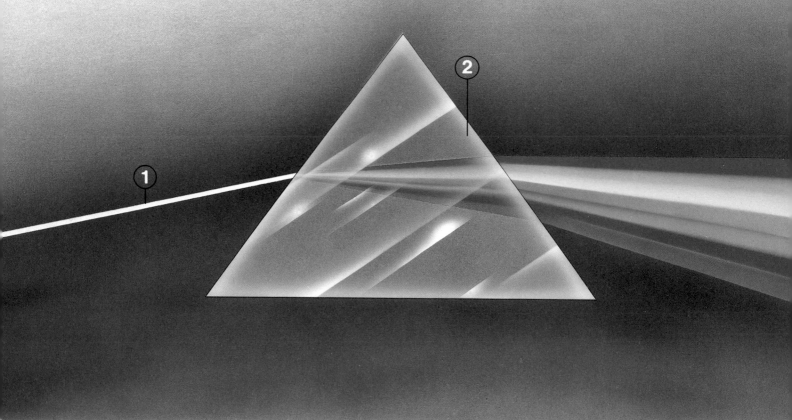

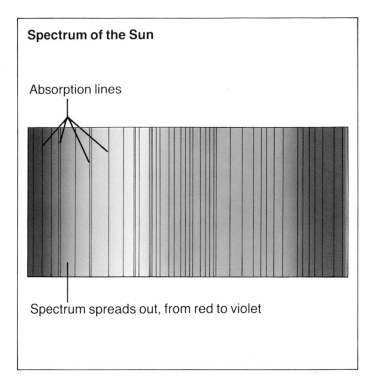

Spectrum of the Sun

Absorption lines

Spectrum spreads out, from red to violet

◁ When you pass "white" light (**1**) through a prism (**2**), it spreads out into a spectrum (**3**) of the wavelengths (colours) making it up.

△ The Sun's spectrum consists of a rainbow crossed by dark lines. These absorption lines come from gases in the Sun's surface layers.

So far, we've thought of light as being a single entity. But like a chord played on a piano, light itself is a mixture of different "notes", or wavelengths. You can see this by spreading out sunlight with a prism, or by looking at reflections off metallic jewelry. When it's spread out, "white" light reveals itself to be made of a blaze of rainbow colours called a *spectrum*. The colours range from violet and blue (shortest wavelengths) through green, yellow and orange to red (longest wavelengths).

However, not everything that emits light has a rainbow spectrum. Gases — like the glowing vapour in sodium and mercury streetlights — have spectra which are dark, with light emitted in just a few narrow lines. The reason for this lies deep in their atomic make-up and temperature.

◁ By placing a thin prism over the lens of a telescope, astronomers can record the spectra of several stars all at once. This shows the spectra of some of the stars in the Hyades star cluster. If you look carefully, you can see slight differences amongst the spectra. These arise from differences in temperature and chemical composition.

No two spectra are alike; the patterns of lines are as individual as our fingerprints.

When astronomers spread out sunlight and analyze it in detail with a spectroscope, they see a rainbow band crossed by hundreds of dark, vertical lines. The rainbow comes from the Sun's hot interior, while the lines are due to gases in the Sun's cooler surface layers. The lines appear dark because the gases absorb light from the hot layers below, instead of emitting it.

These *absorption lines* reveal the Sun's hidden secrets. By recognizing the telltale patterns, astronomers can discover the Sun's chemical make-up: the mix of gases in its surface layers. The lines also tell how hot the Sun is, and careful measurements even reveal the strength of its magnetic field.

Today, astronomers can unlock the secrets of the Universe by examining the spectra of stars and galaxies. Although the spectrum of a star is much fainter than that of the Sun, it still reveals the star's temperature, its composition, and the speed at which it moves through space. Its spectrum can even reveal whether close, unseen companion stars may lurk nearby.

The lukewarm Universe

When you switch on an old-fashioned electric fire — the kind that has bars — you can feel heat coming out of the elements even before they become hot enough to glow. This heat is radiation, too; although, unlike light, you can't see it. It's longer in wavelength than red light, and so it's called infrared radiation ("below red"). Although infrared radiation is invisible, we can feel it and measure it with detectors.

Many objects in space give out this lukewarm radiation, too. Among them are the surfaces of planets, stars too cool to shine and very young stars buried deep inside dense gas and dust clouds. Infrared radiation may even help to locate big planets hidden in the glare of their parent stars (although astronomers have yet to find any!).

Astronomers study infrared radiation with telescopes very similar to conventional optical telescopes. But because infrared radiation is absorbed by water vapour in the atmosphere, observatories need to be situated on very high mountains, where most of the water vapour is frozen out. One of the best sites is on top of the volcano Mauna Kea in Hawaii. However, some astronomers find it hard to work at a height of 4,200 m (13,800 ft). There's an added problem in that any stray heat in the observatory can swamp the faint signals from space, so all the equipment has to be cooled to subzero temperatures. The life of an infrared astronomer is not a comfortable one!

The best place to carry out infrared astronomy is in space, way above our warm Earth and its troublesome atmosphere. In 1983, the world's first orbiting infrared telescope was launched. IRAS — the Infrared Astronomical Satellite — was a joint project between Britain,

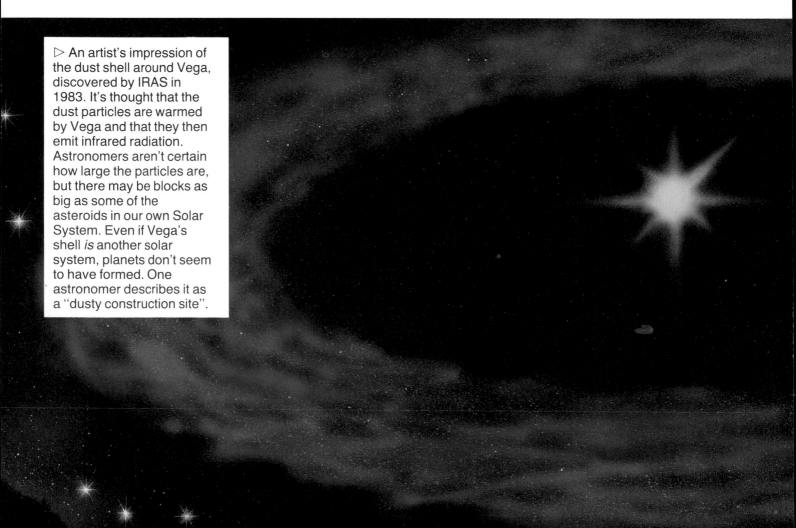

▷ An artist's impression of the dust shell around Vega, discovered by IRAS in 1983. It's thought that the dust particles are warmed by Vega and that they then emit infrared radiation. Astronomers aren't certain how large the particles are, but there may be blocks as big as some of the asteroids in our own Solar System. Even if Vega's shell *is* another solar system, planets don't seem to have formed. One astronomer describes it as a "dusty construction site".

the Netherlands and the United States. It gathered infrared radiation with a mirror 0.6 m (24 in) across. IRAS itself looked rather like a cosmic thermos flask! In order to keep the telescope as cold as possible at −263°C, it was wrapped in an aluminium jacket in which liquid helium circulated. IRAS operated in space for almost a year before its helium coolant ran out.

Scientists are still working on the enormous quantity of data tape sent back by IRAS. It pinpointed over a quarter of a million new infrared sources. Within our Solar System IRAS discovered several new comets, an unusual asteroid which travels close to the Sun, and shells of debris in the asteroid belt. Out in the depths of space IRAS detected a whole new class of galaxies — *starburst galaxies* — whose centres are undergoing a sudden, explosive outburst of starbirth. But, perhaps most exciting of all, was its discovery of shells of dust or debris around some nearby stars, including Vega and Fomalhaut. Some astronomers think that these shells could be made of rocks and asteroids, and that we could be seeing solar systems beyond our own for the first time.

▽ IRAS — seen here surrounded by its liquid helium-cooled aluminium jacket, with trumpet-shaped "sunshade" — was the first orbiting infrared telescope. Circling 900 km (560 miles) above the Earth, it surveyed virtually the whole sky. As well as its more sensational discoveries, IRAS sent back beautiful images of starbirth in action.

Tuning in to the Cosmos

In 1931 an American engineer called Karl Jansky built a huge aerial — it looked like a merry-go-round — to investigate radio disturbances during thunderstorms. To his puzzlement, the aerial picked up radio waves apparently coming from the Milky Way instead. Although he didn't continue his investigations, Jansky had discovered radio astronomy.

Hardly anyone took any notice of his findings until World War II. That's when the Sun's radio waves were discovered, although some people thought the signals were coming from a German secret weapon!

Once the war was over, scientists took advantage of the great strides made in electronics to build equipment for investigating the "radio sky". In the early 1950s Britain led the world in constructing some of the first radio telescopes.

The first radio telescopes were relatively simple. At Cambridge and at Jodrell Bank, near Manchester, astronomers erected wire aerials to pick up radio waves from the sky. As well as radio waves from the Sun and the Milky Way, the astronomers found signals coming from places where stars had blown up, and from galaxies way beyond our own, as well as from areas of the sky where nothing was visible at all.

After the first surveys astronomers started building more sophisticated radio telescopes to look at objects in more detail. That's when the "big dish" aerials began to appear. These work just like optical reflecting telescopes. Radio waves are collected by the dish and focused on to an antenna before being amplified and processed. The main difference is that radio waves are very much longer in wavelength than light. In order to "see" the same amount of

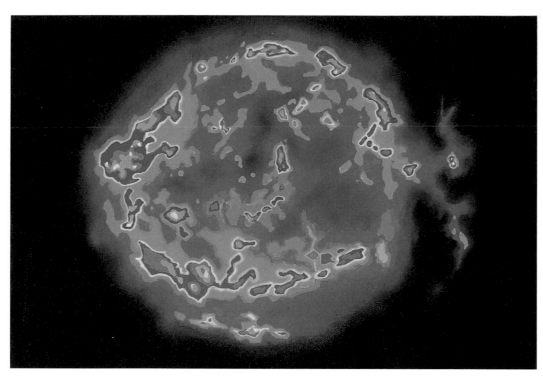

◁ The 76-m (250-ft) dish of the Mark 1A telescope at Jodrell Bank. The telescope has been extensively modernized since it was built in 1957.

△ Radio "photograph" of Cas A, the remains of a star that exploded 300 years ago. Optical telescopes show only wisps of gas in this region.

▽ Karl Jansky's "merry-go-round" was the first telescope to detect cosmic radio waves. It ran on wheels from a Model-T Ford.

detail that an optical telescope sees, radio telescopes need to be very large indeed.

One of the first "big dish" telescopes to be constructed (and still one of the largest in the world) is the Mark IA instrument at Jodrell Bank. The telescope has a dish 76 m (250 ft) in diameter, and is a local landmark. It became famous in 1957 when, newly built, it tracked the first Russian Sputnik as it circled the Earth.

Nowadays the world's largest fully steerable radio dish is the 100-m (300-ft) telescope in Effelsberg, West Germany. But even this is dwarfed by the colossal (but immobile) 305-m (1,000-ft) Arecibo Radio Telescope, which lies in a natural limestone hollow in Puerto Rico.

These giant radio dishes "see" a different — and often more violent — Universe than the one we know. But you don't always need a sophisticated dish to explore the radio sky. One of the most important events in radio astronomy was the discovery of *pulsars* in 1967. These superdense, shrunken neutron stars — which can spin many times a second — were first detected with a simple array of wires strewn over a 4-acre field in Cambridge!

A telescope bigger than Earth

Although radio dishes are built as big as possible, they can never be large enough. To "see" the fine detail revealed by optical telescopes would require a radio dish several kilometres across. And, from an engineering point of view, this isn't possible.

Fortunately, there are ways around the problem. Cambridge radio astronomers hit on a solution in the 1960s when they invented *aperture synthesis*. This involves "synthesizing" an enormous radio dish by combining the output from several smaller ones, arranged in a line. By changing the spacing of the separate telescopes, you can gradually "construct" a radio dish as wide as the line is long. The Cambridge astronomers began this kind of work with an array 1 km long. Today, the eight dishes of the Five-Kilometre Telescope are a prominent feature of the flat Fens landscape.

Now that powerful computers and reliable electronics are readily available, many radio observatories are linking up their single dishes to make arrays. The astronomers at Jodrell Bank have linked up their Mark 1A telescope with five dishes strung along the length of the Welsh Borders. The array is known as the Multi-Element Radio-Linked Interferometer Network, or MERLIN for short!

At present the world's most impressive array of radio telescopes can be found in America. In a dusty, dry lake bed in New Mexico 27 huge dishes, arranged in a Y-shape, make detailed observations of distant radio sources every night and day. For obvious reasons, it's called the Very Large Array (VLA)!

But to see the finest details of all, radio astronomers use a technique called VLBI (Very Long Baseline Interferometry). This involves linking up radio telescopes over huge distances even across oceans. In this way astronomers can peer right into the hearts of objects like radio galaxies and quasars, where it is suspected that giant black holes may lurk.

For the future, many new ultra-sensitive arrays are planned, including nationwide networks in both America and Australia. But the ultimate is QUASAT — an orbiting radio telescope. When QUASAT is linked with ground-based dishes, it will create a radio telescope bigger than the Earth itself.

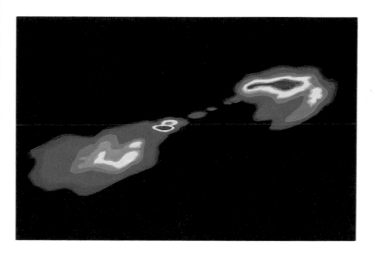

△ This colour-coded VLA image shows the centre of the galaxy Centaurus A. Here, a jet of hot gas emerges from the galaxy's exploding nucleus.

▽ QUASAT, a joint American-European project is due to be launched into orbit by the Space Shuttle in the 1990s.

Astronomy from orbit

When you pick up a suntan on holiday, your body is reacting to radiation on the violet-blue side of the visible spectrum. It's called ultraviolet or uv radiation, meaning "beyond violet". Ultraviolet rays may give you a tan, but, as anyone who's ever suffered sunburn will agree, they are not all good news!

In fact, uv radiation is extremely harmful. It can cause changes in body cells which can lead to skin cancer, and larger doses can kill cells altogether. Fortunately, the Earth's atmosphere contains a "sunscreen" which protects us from most of the Sun's harmful uv rays. A layer of ozone — a form of oxygen gas — absorbs nearly all the short-wavelength uv radiation.

Since so little uv radiation penetrates our atmosphere, astronomers studying it have to send their instruments up into space. There have been two uv satellites: the American Copernicus and the European-American International Ultraviolet Explorer (IUE), which is still in orbit and working well. Neither satellite sent back pictures of the sky as such; both were designed to look at the spectra of objects emitting uv rays. Among these objects are very hot stars, atmospheres around stars, and quasars — galaxies with violent centres.

Shorter in wavelength, and even more energetic than uv rays, are X-rays. As everyone knows, X-rays penetrate flesh with no difficulty at all. It's just as well that those coming from space are blocked by the atmosphere!

Cosmic X-rays were first detected by rockets in the 1960s. Although some X-ray astronomy is still carried out with rockets and high-flying balloons, most research is done with satellites. The satellites UHURU, Einstein and Exosat have all sent back information on the X-ray Universe. They have even returned stunning pictures — which is all the more remarkable, when you consider that X-rays would go straight through a conventional telescope and out the other side! To "see" X-rays, astronomers have had to design special telescopes in which the rays come in at such shallow angles that they're not absorbed.

X-rays come from some of the fiercest, most energetic environments in the Universe. By studying them, astronomers can learn about regions as bizarre as the neighbourhood of a pulsar — or the throat of a black hole.

▷ Cosmic tug-of-war: the immense gravity of a collapsed neutron star tears off its companion's outer layers. The violently heated gas emits X-rays as it spirals down on to the neutron star's surface.

▽ **IUE satellite:**
1 Solar panels for power
2 Main body of satellite
3 Guide tube for uv radiation on to 0.45-m (18-in) diameter telescope

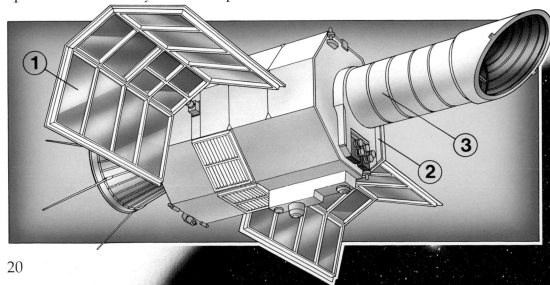

High-energy astronomy

The most violent and energetic events in space give rise to the most exotic radiations of all: gamma rays and cosmic rays.

Gamma rays are a form of electromagnetic radiation, but they are shorter in wavelength and more energetic even than X-rays. They manage to penetrate our atmosphere to some extent, which means that they can be studied by instruments carried up on balloons, but luckily they can't reach the ground.

Some of the first discoveries in gamma-ray astronomy were made by American spy satellites. Monitoring the Earth for secret nuclear tests, the satellites detected bursts of gamma rays coming from the sky instead. These are now believed to come from distant neutron stars.

But gamma-ray astronomy is only just beginning. Although some double stars, and possibly the centre of our Galaxy, have been identified as being gamma-ray sources, there is a great deal more to discover. Only one satellite — Europe's COS-B — has so far made a proper survey of cosmic gamma rays.

If you want to find cosmic rays, you *don't* use a satellite: you would never pick up enough of them! Cosmic rays fan out as they collide with particles in our atmosphere. To catch the greatest number, cosmic ray "telescopes" must cover areas dozens of hectares across. And, just to confuse the issue, cosmic rays aren't actually rays at all, but energetic streams of protons (positively charged subatomic particles). They come from violent regions of space: from the exploded remains of stars, from close double stars tearing one another apart and from the centres of exploding galaxies.

◁ Because gamma rays can penetrate down through the atmosphere to heights of about 50 km (30 miles), they can be detected with equipment carried on a balloon. Here, a helium-filled balloon prepares for launch.

▷ These wispy filaments in Vela are all you can see of a star that exploded 11,000 years ago. But at high energies, you can easily detect the star's corpse — a collapsed neutron star that spins 13 times a second.

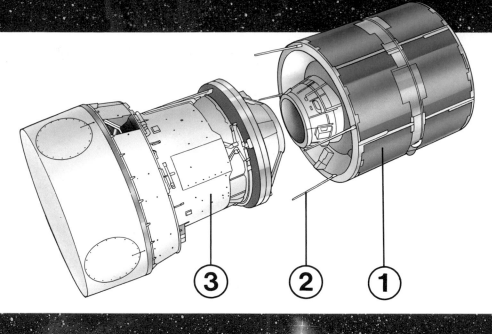

◁ **COS-B satellite**
1 Solar cells wrapped around body of satellite; all the detectors lie inside.
2 Communications antennae.
3 Final stage booster rocket to put satellite into orbit.

COS-B operated between 1975 and 1982 and is the only satellite to have surveyed the gamma-ray sky. American and Soviet–French gamma-ray satellites will soon be observing the sky in more detail.

Unusual observatories

Half a century ago, most observatories were just collections of telescope domes huddled together on high mountains. But now that astronomers are taking advantage of all the "windows" on the Universe available to them, their observatories to look anything but conventional.

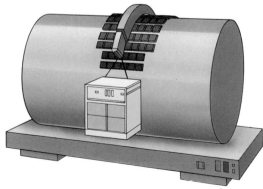

△ Dozens of aluminium cylinders like this one — spread far and wide across the countryside — make up a gravitational-wave detector.

One of the world's most dramatic observatories is on Puerto Rico. There, in a natural limestone bowl surrounded by jungle, lies the world's largest radio telescope: the 305-m (1,000ft) diameter Arecibo dish. The dish itself can't be moved, but the antenna — suspended 130 m (425 ft) above — has a track on which detectors can travel, giving coverage of the sky overhead.

From the spectacular setting of Arecibo, it's a long way to the next kind of observatory: a collection of aluminium cylinders scattered across the United States. These make up a gravitational-wave telescope.

Gravitational waves exist only in theory. They *should* be emitted (as a "ripple" in space) whenever a massive body is disturbed — like a star falling into a black hole, for example. Heavy metal bars on Earth — spaced wide apart, to avoid confusion with local disturbances — should then respond by vibrating simultaneously.

Despite false alarms, no gravitational waves have yet been detected. Only time, and more sensitive "telescopes", will tell if they exist.

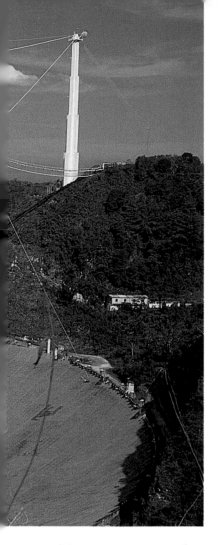

◁ The world's biggest radio telescope — the 305-m (1,000-ft) diameter Arecibo dish — lies amongst the jungles of Puerto Rico.

△ This 1,000,000-gallon tank — filled with a chemical similar to cleaning fluid — detects neutrinos coming from nuclear reactions which take place at the Sun's core. To protect it from other radiations, the tank is buried 1.6 km (1 mile) underground in a gold mine.

▽ Like futuristic beehives, the telescopes in the CERGA interferometer array cluster on a mountainside above Nice. The array will be partly used to measure the diameters of stars.

Neutrinos certainly exist. They are massless, chargeless particles produced in nuclear reactions, like those that power the Sun. They wing away from the Sun's core at the speed of light, giving inside information on its powerhouse. And astronomers have set up the world's most peculiar observatory to catch them — a huge tank filled with a chemical like cleaning fluid, which reacts when a neutrino passes through it. The tank is buried deep in a goldmine to screen it from other forms of radiation.

But the neutrinos are going missing. The tank isn't registering nearly as many as we would expect — something which is making astronomers think twice about what makes the Sun shine.

In the chill mountains above Nice in France is another strange observatory. It looks more like a cluster of beehives! In fact, it's an array of optical telescopes called an *interferometer*. Like an array of radio telescopes, it can "see" more detail than an individual telescope. The array will be used to "split" close double stars and measure star diameters.

Photographing the sky

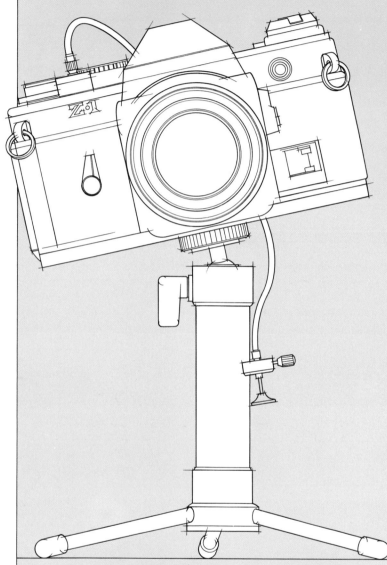

Making a camera mount

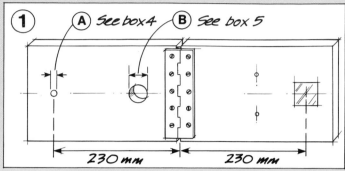

1 Join two equal-sized pieces of plywood (each about 300 mm long) with a hinge. In one piece, drill a hole (**A**) about 230 mm from the hinge, and a second hole (**B**) as shown. Glue a metal square on to the other piece 230 mm from the hinge.

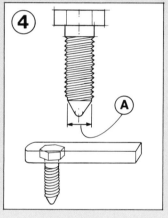

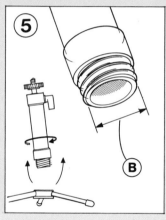

4 You need a bolt, size 0BA. Hole **A** must equal its diameter. Attach a handle to the top of the bolt, so you can turn it.

5 You need a mini-tripod: hole **B** must equal the diameter of the screw that you find when you remove the tripod from its base.

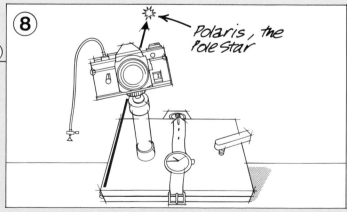

8 On a clear night, set up the camera on a horizontal surface such as a table top—the spirit level will help you check. Find the Pole Star. Sight along the hinge, and rotate the whole mounting until the hinge is lined up with the Pole Star.

You can take sky photographs with an ordinary camera, as long as it has a setting marked B which lets you keep the shutter open. To keep the camera steady, you must put it on a tripod and use a cable release. You will also need some fast film (400 ASA or more). Point the camera at the sky for a few minutes, and you will get a photograph—but the stars will be stretched into streaks because the Earth is rotating. This simple camera mount counteracts the turning of the Earth to give you sharp pictures of the sky.

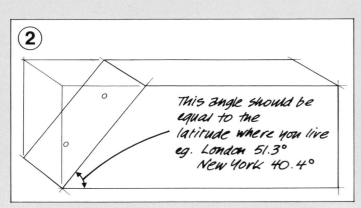

2 Find a block of wood that is roughly 80 × 60 mm in cross-section and about 400 mm long. Use a protractor to mark an angle equal to your latitude on the sides of the block, and carefully cut off the end of the block at this angle.

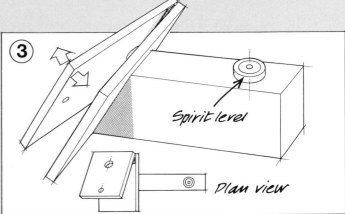

3 Attach the hinged plywood pieces to the sawn-off end of the block, with two screws through the plywood piece that carries the metal square. If you like, you can stick a spirit level on the block, to make sure everything is level.

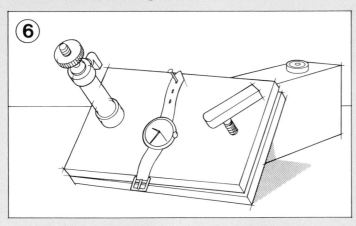

6 Screw the bolt halfway into hole **A**, so it pushes against the metal square. Screw the mini-tripod firmly into hole **B**. Find a watch with a rotating second hand (*not* a digital watch), and hang it from a small nail knocked into the board.

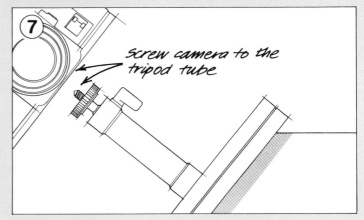

7 Screw the camera on to the top of the mini-tripod. Make sure that the whole assembly does not tip over: if it does, you need a longer or heavier base block. Fit a cable-release to the camera to operate the shutter without shaking it.

9 *Without moving the mount at all,* swivel the camera on top of the mini-tripod, until it points toward the stars that you want to photograph. Wind on the film and make sure that the camera exposure is on the B setting.

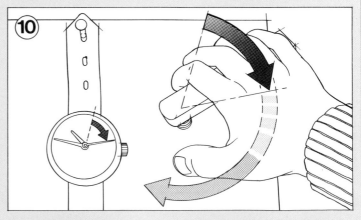

10 Press the cable release, and lock it. At once, start turning the handle on the bolt *at exactly the same pace as the second hand on the watch.* Continue until the exposure is complete, then unlock the cable release.

Choosing a telescope

Buying a telescope is an expensive business. So before you part with your savings, make sure you're ready for one — that you know the sky well enough to be able to put a telescope to good use. If in doubt, buy a pair of binoculars instead; those marked 7×50 or 10×50 will give excellent views of the night sky. When you do get round to buying a telescope, you come up against the next problem: which kind to choose…

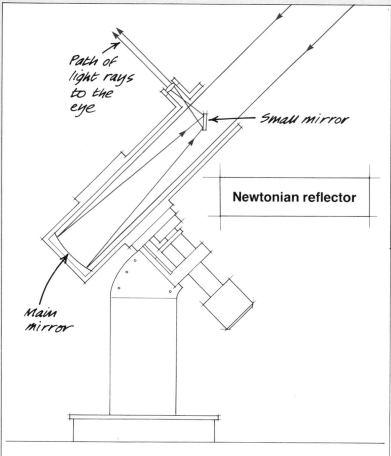

Path of light rays to the eye

Small mirror

Newtonian reflector

Main mirror

◁ Reflecting telescopes collect light with a concave mirror. In the most common kind — the Newtonian reflector — the light is then reflected off a plane mirror (the "flat") into an eyepiece at the side of the tube which enlarges the image. Most serious amateurs prefer reflectors, partly because you can have as big a mirror as you can afford, and this gives the best light-grasp.

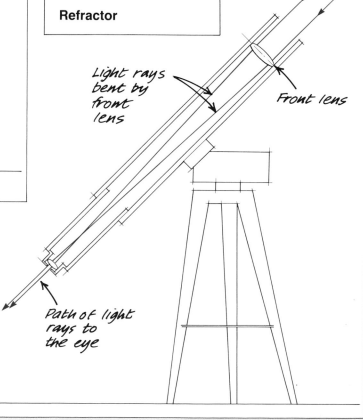

Refractor

Light rays bent by front lens

Front lens

Path of light rays to the eye

▷ Refractors gather light with a lens (or, more usually, a combination of lenses to cut down on the "false colour" that lenses naturally produce). Although refractors are more portable and need less upkeep than reflectors, their light-grasp isn't usually as good (and lenses more than 10 cm across are extremely expensive). But refractors are very good for casual stargazing and introducing beginners to the "feel" of a telescope.

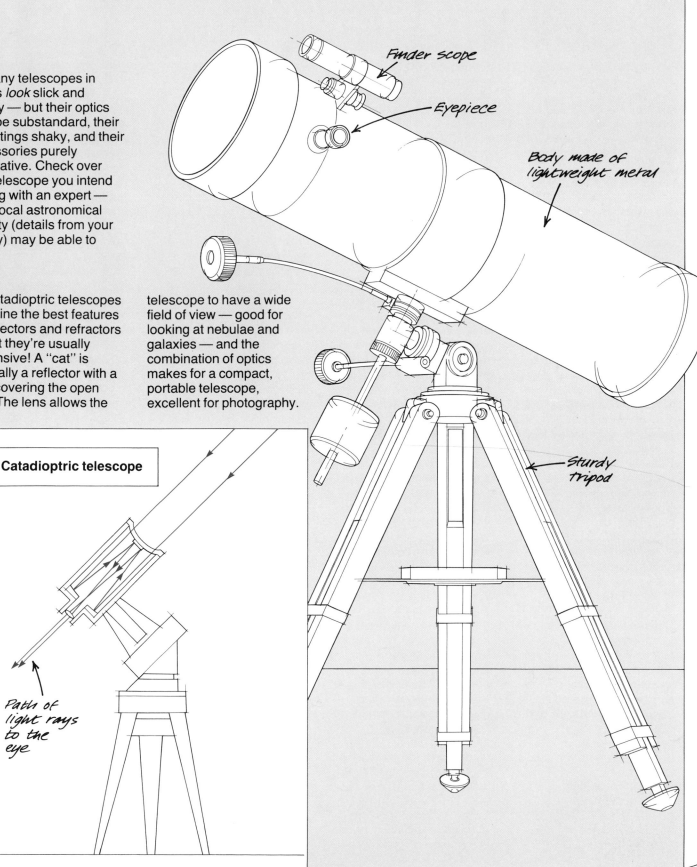

Finder scope

Eyepiece

Body made of lightweight metal

Sturdy Tripod

▷ Many telescopes in shops *look* slick and glossy — but their optics may be substandard, their mountings shaky, and their accessories purely decorative. Check over any telescope you intend buying with an expert — your local astronomical society (details from your library) may be able to help.

▽ Catadioptric telescopes combine the best features of reflectors and refractors — but they're usually expensive! A "cat" is basically a reflector with a lens covering the open end. The lens allows the telescope to have a wide field of view — good for looking at nebulae and galaxies — and the combination of optics makes for a compact, portable telescope, excellent for photography.

Catadioptric telescope

Path of light rays to the eye

Glossary

Absorption line Narrow zone in the spectrum of a gas where light is absorbed. A gas's spectral lines are its "fingerprint"; they allow astronomers to find out what the Sun and stars are made of.

Aperture synthesis Technique used in radio astronomy in which several separate radio dishes are combined electronically to "synthesize" one very big dish. It allows astronomers to see very fine detail.

Black hole A region of space where the pull of gravity is so great that not even light can escape.

Catadioptric telescope Telescope that gathers light with a combinaton of lenses and mirrors. A "cat" is a compact portable telescope with a wide field of view.

Charge-coupled device (CCD) A light-sensitive silicon chip used in electronic detectors to give pictures of objects in the sky. A CCD is about 30 times more sensitive than a photographic plate, which means that long exposure times are no longer needed.

Colour-coding Technique which uses colour to highlight different regions of an image. The colours — which are usually computer-generated and bear no resemblance to the object's real colours — can be used to show differences in brightness, temperature, etc.

Cosmic rays Highly energetic particles which bombard the Earth from space. Most are protons (positively charged particles) which come from the remains of exploded stars.

Electromagnetic spectrum Waves made up of electric and magnetic vibrations, which travel through space at the speed of light. They range from long-wavelength radio waves, through light, to short-wavelength gamma rays.

Eyepiece Small lens placed at the viewing end of a telescope to magnify the image produced by the mirror or main lens.

"False colour" Unwanted colour produced by a lens. It is caused by the lens acting like a prism and splitting the light up into a rainbow spectrum.

Focus Point in a telescope where rays gathered by the lens or mirror converge; the place where the image of the object being viewed is formed.

Gamma rays Extremely short-wavelength radiation. Gamma rays are also the most energetic rays in the whole electromagnetic spectrum.

Gravitational waves Very weak waves that are believed to be produced when massive bodies are disturbed. So far, no gravitational waves have been detected.

Image intensifier Electronic tube, which converts a faint light signal from a telescope into a bright electronic picture.

Infrared radiation Radiation with a wavelength longer than red light but shorter than radio waves. On Earth, we encounter it as heat.

Light Radiation that our eyes are sensitive to. Light is made up of a narrow band of wavelengths, which we perceive as colours.

Neutrino Sub-atomic particle without mass or charge, sometimes produced in nuclear reactions. Because they are virtually unstoppable, neutrinos stream away directly into space from the Sun's core (where its nuclear power source lies). By monitoring the Sun's neutrinos, astronomers hope to learn more about its energy production.

Neutron star A collapsed star composed mainly of neutrons. Pulsars are young, fast-spinning neutron stars.

Ozone layer A form of oxygen gas that makes up a layer in Earth's atmosphere. It acts as a sunscreen, blocking most of the ultraviolet radiation coming from space.

Photoelectric effect Effect that takes place when a beam of radiation hits certain metals. The radiation ejects electrons (negatively charged particles) from the surface. These stream away as an electric current, which can then be measured.

Photomultiplier tube A detector that converts light into an electric current through the photoelectric effect, and then greatly amplifies the signal. It means that even a faint star can produce a detectable signal.

Prism A block of glass or perspex that disperses a beam of light into a rainbow spectrum.

Quasar A brilliant, tiny object further away than most of the galaxies. Quasars are probably the cores of young active galaxies, whose outer regions are too distant and faint to be easily seen.

Radio waves Radiation that has the longest wavelengths of all. Most radio waves penetrate our atmosphere and can be picked up by radio telescopes.

Reflecting telescope Telescope that gathers light with a concave mirror.

Refracting telescope Telescope which collects light with a combination of lenses.

Schmidt telescope A catadioptric telescope designed to be used for photography alone.

Spectroscope An instrument used to break up light into its separate wavelengths.

Spectrum The result of splitting up light from a source into its separate wavelengths. Very hot, dense objects (like the main body of the Sun) have a rainbow spectrum. Less-dense gases (like those in the Sun's atmosphere) emit or absorb light only at certain wavelengths.

Starburst galaxy A galaxy with an active core which looks at first sight like a Seyfert galaxy or a quasar. However, the disturbance is probably due to a sudden burst of star formation.

Ultraviolet (uv) radiation Radiation shorter in wavelength than blue light, which can cause sunburn. Most ultraviolet radiation is absorbed by the ozone layer.

Unsharp masking Technique used in astronomical photography in which the original photograph is re-shot through a negative "mask" of itself. This tones down the strong contrasts in the original, and allows fine details to show through.

Finding out more

VLBI Very Long Baseline Interferometry — a way of "seeing" the finest details in radio sources, by electronically linking up telescopes separated by thousands of kilometres.
Wavelength The distance from crest to crest of any wave motion, such as radiation. All radiations travel at the speed of light; but short-wavelength radiations vibrate more rapidly and pack more energy than do long-wavelength radiations.
X-rays Very short-wavelength, highly penetrating radiation. X-rays from space come from violent places, like the region around a black hole.

Many observatories are now open to the public, and a few even have telescopes you can look through yourself. But if you're really keen to buy or make a telescope of your own, the best way to get expert help and advice is by joining an astronomical society.

There are two main societies for amateur astronomers in the UK, and both of these have many members who live abroad.

▽ The 70-mm (28-in) telescope at Greenwich is the largest refractor (lens telescope) in the UK. It is part of the Old Royal Observatory founded in 1675. The Observatory — now a museum — is open to the public all year round.

The best for beginners is the Junior Astronomical Society. You can get a joining form by writing to Martin Ratcliffe, 36 Fairway, Keyworth, Nottingham NG12 5DU. The British Astronomical Association (Burlington House, Piccadilly, London W1V 9AG) caters for amateurs who are more advanced. If you'd rather join a society a bit closer to home, the UK has hundreds of local societies and clubs. There's a new list of these published every year in Patrick Moore's Yearbook of Astronomy (Sidgwick & Jackson).

Astronomical societies often run courses which cover aspects of telescope making. And there are many other courses in which you're encouraged to bring telescopes along. In this way, you get the chance to try out several telescopes to find the one that suits you.

You'll find that astronomical societies carry advertisements for telescopes in their magazines. Some of these telescopes will be secondhand, and you *can* pick up a bargain (but test out the telescope thoroughly first). Commercial telescope manufacturers also advertise here; but since their addresses always seem to be changing, it's best to refer to a current magazine for up-to-date information.

If you're interested in what professional astronomers do, there are several museums and observatories where you can find out. There are two Royal Observatories: the Royal Greenwich Observatory, Herstmonceux Castle, E. Sussex (open in summer), and the Royal Observatory, Blackford Hill, Edinburgh (open all year). If you're interested in the history of the telescope, there's the Old Royal Observatory at Greenwich, London's Science Museum, and Merseyside County Museums in Liverpool; and radio astronomy enthusiasts musn't miss out on a visit to Jodrell Bank in Cheshire.

Because of Britain's cloudy climate, not many observatories have "public telescopes". But if you're in Scotland or Northern Ireland, and the sky happens to be clear, get in touch with either the Mills Observatory (Balgay Hill, Dundee, Scotland) or the Armagh Planetarium (College Hill, Armagh, N. Ireland), and ask if they plan to demonstrate any of their telescopes that night.

In Australia, there are two major observatories in New South Wales you should visit. There's the Anglo-Australian Observatory at Siding Spring, which houses the 3.9-m Anglo-Australian Telescope and the 1.2-m UK Schmidt; and the Parkes Observatory (at Parkes) with its giant 64-m radio dish.

Index

PRINTED IN BELGIUM BY
proost
INTERNATIONAL BOOK PRODUCTION